Teeth

Written by Kath Beattie

raintree
a Capstone company — publishers for children

Lots of living things have teeth. There are three main sorts of teeth – **flat teeth**, **sharp teeth** and **pointed teeth**.

Flat teeth mash green food into little bits. A cow's main teeth are flat teeth to chomp with. She has some sharp teeth to cut off greens, too.

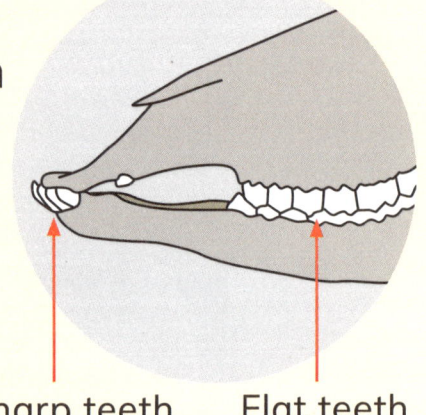

Sharp teeth   Flat teeth

Pointed teeth are 'fangs'. Fangs come in pairs. Hunters have fangs. Fangs rip food into shreds. A fox has 2 pairs of fangs. He rips his food and gulps it down. He has no flat teeth.

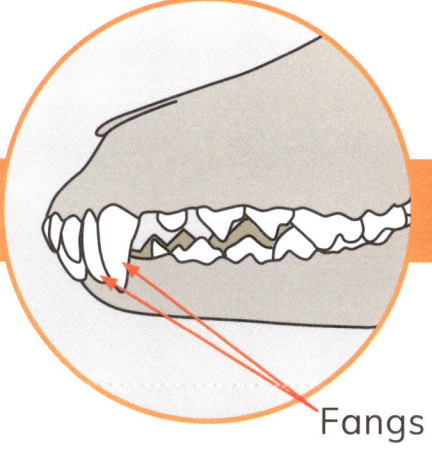
Fangs

A raccoon has all three sorts of teeth.

Dragonfish

The dragonfish is just a little fish, but it has big killer teeth. They are sharp and hooked. It swims deep, deep down in the dark. But it has a light that comes out from its lips. This light helps it get a fish for dinner. The fish that it is hunting sees the light and swims up to it.

Then, the dragonfish turns its light to red. Fish cannot see red. So the dragonfish **snaps** its teeth shut on the fish in the dark! Its teeth form a trap. Now the fish cannot get out. The dragonfish has its dinner.
It is a clever killer with big sharp teeth.

Big cats

Big cats have sharp teeth and 2 pairs of pointed fangs. They are hunters. They rip food. They have no flat teeth at all.

Look at this big cat's 4 pointed fangs. She is a top hunter. She can kill an elk with one big crunch.

Toothed stag

This stag comes out at dusk. He is a bit odd as he chomps on greens, but he has a pair of long fangs. His fangs are not for ripping food. They are for fighting stags. As well as his fangs, he has flat teeth for munching on greens.

Rats

Rats have 12 flat teeth and 4 sharp teeth. The sharp teeth never stop getting bigger. A rat has to crunch on hard things, like wood, to keep the teeth short and sharp. Rats like lots of foods, such as nuts and seeds.

Sharp teeth

Kangaroos

A kangaroo has 8 sharp teeth and 26 flat teeth. The sharp teeth are at the tip – 6 at the top, and 2 on the bottom. Then there is a gap, and the flat teeth are at the back of the cheeks.

Flat teeth

Sharp teeth

A kangaroo cuts off green food with the sharp teeth and puts it in the gap. The kangaroo pushes it bit by bit to the flat cheek teeth. Then kangaroos look like they are chomping gum. But they are just munching the greens into shreds. It's a long job.

When a flat tooth gets old and drops out, the next flat tooth in the cheek shifts along to fill the gap. Clever!

Zebra

You can see zebra in Africa.
Zebra have flat teeth and sharp teeth. The sharp teeth rip up green food, such as shrubs and bark. The flat teeth mash it into bits.
Zebra have 40 teeth. Some dad zebra have extra teeth to fight with.

Zebra roam far to get food. They travel in a pack, keeping a look out for the big cats that might hunt them.

Crocs

A croc has 60 to 100 sharp teeth and some fangs. A croc never runs out of teeth. When a tooth drops out, a fresh one appears.

A croc's teeth are for grabbing food. He drags the food down deep to drown it. He rips it into big bits and gulps it down. Then he has a rest!

This croc looks as if he is grinning in his sleep. But he is fooling you. If you go up to him, he will **snap**. And that will be the end of you!

A croc's teeth do up like a zip.

The boss of the woods

The boss is **big** with thick brown fur. She has 42 teeth – a mix of flat teeth (26), sharp teeth (12) and 4 pointed fangs.

She needs a lot of food as she sleeps all winter in a den.

She is a good hunter. She kills sheep and elk with her fangs. She rips bark with her fangs to get bugs. She gets nuts, roots, fish and rats. And she can crush greens with her flat teeth, too.

The boss loves to fish.

Killer sharks

Killer sharks have lots and lots of pointed teeth. They are not fangs. The teeth do not have roots. So, when the killer shark chomps on food, some teeth might fall out. But she is clever – fresh teeth soon pop up. An old shark will have popped up a lot of teeth – up to 30,000!

Sharks with little teeth

This sort of shark has 3,000 sharp teeth. But do not panic, she will not kill you. Her food is little fish, like shrimp and krill. Her teeth are little, too.

Honk!

This one has 32 teeth and 4 big 'tusks'. Tusks look like fangs, but they are not for ripping food. Her tusks are for fighting for her little ones. The flat teeth at the back of her cheeks are for crushing her greens. Her teeth keep getting bigger and bigger. She keeps them sharp and short by chomping on things.

Tusks

Flat teeth

Can you see him in the river? He likes to float here. He loves greens so he will not kill to get food. But look out, as he will fight if you get too near.

Orca

An orca is as big as a bus. She looks chilling. She is stunning! She has 40 to 48 teeth. No one has teeth as sharp as her. She is the top hunter as she is not hunted at all.

An orca chomps on all sorts of things. She might chomp on your boat. But an orca will not chomp on you!

The tooth duck

The Goosander (or 'tooth duck') looks like she has lots of sharp teeth. But they are not proper teeth. They are little, hard points on her long, thin bill. The teeth let the Goosander grip a fish hard so it cannot get free. Clever duck!